THE MATT MERTON MYSTERIES

Teacher's Book

Catherine Gilhooly

Rising Stars UK Ltd
7 Hatchers Mews, Bermondsey Street, London SE1 3GS
www.risingstars-uk.com

NASEN House, 4/5 Amber Business Village, Amber Close,
Amington, Tamworth, Staffordshire B77 4RP

Text, design and layout © Rising Stars UK Ltd.

The right of Catherine Gilhooly to be identified as the author of this work has been asserted by her in accordance with the Copyright, Design and Patents Act 1988.

Published 2010
Reprinted 2011

Text, design and layout © Rising Stars UK Ltd.

Cover design: pentacor**big**
Text design and typesetting: Clive Sutherland
Publisher: Gill Budgell
Editorial consultant: Lorraine Petersen

All rights reserved. No part of this publication may be reproduced, stored in a retrieval system, or transmitted in any form by any means, electronic, mechanical, photocopying, recording or otherwise without the prior permission of Rising Stars UK Ltd, except where photocopying for educational purposes within the school or other educational establishment that has purchased this book is expressly permitted in the text.

British Library Cataloguing in Publication Data.
A CIP record for this book is available from the British Library.

ISBN: 978-1-84680-802-9

Printed by Ashford Colour Press Ltd.

Contents

Introduction to *The Matt Merton Mysteries*	4
Ways of working effectively with *The Matt Merton Mysteries*, including strategies on Guided Reading	5
Some light touch phonics work	7
The importance of good questioning in guided reading	8
The Matt Merton Mysteries eBooks	8
Deadly Night	9
Set Up	12
The Warning	15
The Nightmare	18
The Trap	21
Changing Sides	24
The End: Part 1	27
The End: Part 2	30

Introduction to *The Matt Merton Mysteries*

There are eight books in *The Matt Merton Mysteries* series. They follow on from the *Shadows* series, in which the character Matt Merton is introduced, along with the basic plot – Matt is working for an organisation called The Firm, fighting against aliens that have landed on Earth. The stories can be read in isolation as each has its own stand-alone plot and resolution. However, there are developments throughout the series as Matt finds out more and more about his situation. Each book has the same four introductory pages which set the scene for the reader. These explain the background to the story and give some key information about Matt Merton.

A sensible reading order for the series would be to start with *Deadly Night*, *Set Up*, *The Warning*, *The Nightmare* and *The Trap*. In these books Matt discovers that The Firm was in fact created by the aliens to assist them in taking over the world. He realises that The Firm are killing innocent people and also trying to kill him because he knows the truth about them. In *Changing Sides* Matt finally makes contact with his missing girlfriend, Jane, and they agree to join forces to fight the aliens and The Firm. The series reaches a climax with *The End: Parts 1* and *2* in which Matt and his allies defeat the aliens.

Well-drawn characters

Matt Merton is the central character of the series. He works for a shadowy organisation called The Firm, under whose orders he seeks out and kills 'The Enemy' with his Truth Stick. Filled with doubts about the ethics of his actions, he broods in the shadows of his local cafe. His main motivation is to find his missing girlfriend, Jane.

There are three strongly drawn secondary characters. Sam, the cafe owner, is reluctantly drawn into the story action through his friendship with Matt. He is torn between his fear of The Firm and his desire to support his friend.

Matt's work partner, Dexter, is dedicated to The Firm and has no qualms about killing people. He often accuses Matt of being too soft and not committed to the job. As the series unfolds, it turns out that Dexter is trying to kill Matt.

Jane, Matt's girlfriend, has coordinated a resistance movement against the aliens and formed a plan to overthrow them. She resists contacting Matt until she knows he has turned his back on The Firm. She bravely leads Matt and Sam into the aliens' headquarters to fight them.

Motivating story lines

Central to the plots of *The Matt Merton Mysteries* is a sense of darkness and foreboding. The Firm bill themselves as the respected heroes, keeping the streets safe from alien encroachment. In their daily work, Matt and Dexter are supposedly seeking out and intercepting aliens, who are in human form, and then terminating them. But as the books progress, the reader cannot help but feel Matt's increasing anxiety that this is just a cover story for an evil alliance between The Firm and the alien invaders.

Matt has a nightmare that suggests the aliens created The Firm and he keeps having near-misses in which The Firm send him on assignments where he nearly gets killed. He begins to suspect that his colleague Dexter is part of the plot against him and all these factors add to the increasing tension. Matt finally finds Jane and she confirms the real truth about The Firm and the aliens' plans to end the human race and take over the world. Matt and Jane decide to embark on a high-risk plan to attack the aliens' headquarters. Along the way, Matt has some frightening experiences with the alien leader, before they meet for a final showdown.

The Matt Merton Mysteries, along with its predecessor *Shadows*, are science fiction thriller series. They are set in a bleak future with grey skies and constant snow and rain, throughout both winter and summer. In many ways they were influenced by George Orwell's classic novel *1984*, Ridley Scott's atmospheric film *Blade Runner* and more recently, the Jason Bourne trilogy.

Supportive teacher resources

Each story is supported by a range of activities. In addition to a story summary, the teacher's book includes questions for the teacher to ask in order to interrogate the text and develop the pupils' comprehension.

There are drama and role-play suggestions which help the pupils understand and empathise with the characters and their situations. These can be good preliminary activities for pupils attempting to understand motivation and how characters think and act prior to further analysis.

Word and text level suggestions are provided for each story based on the words and language structures used. Discussion should take place in a guided reading activity as to how the author achieves effects both on the page and in the mind of the reader.

There are two photocopy master activities for each story. The photocopy masters focus on characterisation, comprehension, empathy and prediction – all of which will help in the guided reading process. Suggestions for the development or adaptation of the activities are provided on the teacher's page.

Opportunities for writing

It is often assumed, wrongly, that reluctant readers are also reluctant writers. The photocopy master activities in this teacher's book are designed to give pupils substantial opportunities for writing. The writing activities in the photocopy masters can be used flexibly by the teacher, depending on the time available. Pupils can either write on the photocopiable sheets or they can develop their ideas on a separate sheet of paper.

The 'Talk about' extension activity is about developing the idea on the sheet, or can be used for initiating writing or further discussion.

In-built differentiation

The teaching resource materials offer teachers opportunities for differentiation.

- The text interrogation questions cater for a range of abilities.
- The photocopy master activities can be used in a variety of ways to suit a pupil's needs and abilities. Teachers can blank out sections if required. Some pupils could do the extension activity only.
- The role-play suggestions allow pupils to respond to the reading material using differing levels of language and detail.

Assessment Focus charts relating to the photocopy masters

	AF1	AF2	AF3	AF4	AF5	AF6	AF7	AF8
Deadly Night	W		R					
Set Up		R	R	R				
The Warning		W	R W				W	
The Nightmare	W	R	R				W	
The Trap		R	R	R				
Changing Sides		W	R					
The End: Part 1	W	R					W	
The End: Part 2		R W	R W					

R = Reading AF   W = Writing AF

Each photocopy master covers one or two Assessment Foci for either reading or writing or both. You can use this as part of Assessing Pupils' Progress (APP).

Ways of working effectively with the series

The Matt Merton Mysteries series of eight titles is ideal for one to one reading or with a small group.

Because each of the books in the series has an average text length of 1300 words and reading age of 7–8 years old, they should be a suitable read for some of the weakest readers at KS3 and above. A book at an appropriate reading level will present the reader with a challenge on no more than ten per cent of words; so the reader should be able to read nine words out of ten comfortably.

Strategies on which to base your Guided Reading

You will often find yourself guiding the reading of a small group of pupils. Any group that has a text such as those in *The Matt Merton Mysteries* as its main reading book will be very vulnerable and in need of much reassurance and support. The following strategies should underpin your reading group sessions with them.

- Build on a pupil's prior knowledge, interests and enthusiasms. Always make this your starting point. A lot of pupils will know about the science fiction genre from television and films. (*Dr Who* and the Jason Bourne films are current favourites). This prior knowledge will boost their confidence, even when their reading skills are weak.
- Use plenty of praise and rewards to boost low self-esteem and gain lesson momentum. (See 'Making the most of praise and rewards' on page 6 for more detail.)
- *The Matt Merton Mysteries* series has a rich tapestry of illustrations within each story. Discuss them with the pupils and look for interesting further information about character, plot and atmosphere, using these visual clues.
- Teach in a small 'step-by-step' approach, so that it's almost impossible for the pupils to feel unsure of what's going on. This is sometimes described as creating an **'error free'** environment.
- Build up your pupils' phonic skills. Most secondary students with literacy problems have sound to letter mapping inadequacies. A light touch with imagination and invention is necessary, or you will destroy the sense of fun and feelings of confidence that are so vital to a successful reading intervention. (See 'Some light touch phonics work' on page 7 for some ideas.)
- Always use a strategy called **over learning.** Your pupils have low levels of confidence from their frequent failures to learn to read well. They need a lot more repetition and reinforcement than others. When reading with them, try to give those opportunities to them.
- If you have set your readers personal targets for their group sessions, then you will need to remind them of where they are at the start of every session. For example, before a pupil reads, you should point out that you want to see them using the strategy of breaking unfamiliar words into their sounds and then blending back together again.

Here are some examples of other good targets for your pupils:
- stop if you make a mistake and take your time before you move on;
- reread a phrase to try and get it right;
- look for a pattern of letters you recognise in the words, or a word within a word. For example, there is 'a rat' in 'separate'; 'repeat' contains the word 'pea';
- use the pictures to help you.

In an effective Guided Reading session pupils will be practising the following:
- talking about the text they are reading;
- predicting how the narrative will develop;
- retelling the story as they go along, describing characters and character interaction;
- using specific language from the text (for example, *The Trap* uses the word 'shrill' which the pupils might not be familiar with);
- reading aloud using the skills of scanning ahead, rereading and self-correcting;
- making inferences about the motivation and attitude of the characters.

Introductory activities
- Read the title on the front cover with the pupils.
- Ask the pupils to find the names of the author and illustrator and perhaps the publisher and ISBN number.
- Ask the pupils to scan through the book to look for clues about the names of the main characters.
- Ask the pupils to look at the pictures and predict what they think the story will be about.
- Ask the pupils to find important or difficult words, practise reading them and work out what they mean.
- Question the pupils about the genre of their text. Is it fiction or non-fiction? Is it crime or mystery? Is it sci-fi or romance? Once the pupils have decided on a genre, do they know what the conventions of that genre are? For example, in the science fiction genre there could be:
  - a setting in the future or another time period;
  - a setting in outer space, or on other worlds, possibly involving aliens;
  - stories that involve discovery or application of new scientific ideas, such as time travel, or a new technology, such as faster-than-light travel or robots, or of new and different groups of beings.

  What examples of new technology can the pupils find in *The Matt Merton Mysteries*? Science fiction often has alien life forms. Are there examples of this in the series?

During 'Reading aloud'
When a pupil gets stuck on a word, encourage them to try some of these strategies to unblock themselves.
- What word would make sense here?
- Does the sentence I have read sound right?
- Is there a picture I can use to guess this word?
- Does the word look like another I know? If so, how would it sound?
- Did I get the right sound at the beginning of the word?
- Can I say the last part of the word correctly?
- Shall I break the word down into its sounds and then roll it back together?

Making the most of praise and rewards
Pupils who are reading *The Matt Merton Mysteries* will need very regular positive reinforcement.

Praise coaxes reluctant readers along, strengthens the important emotional and psychological bond between reader and adult, and creates a good psychological atmosphere for reading aloud to take place.

Praise that links in with a merit system is also useful. Low level, high frequency rewards encourage engagement with a reading lesson. The use of merit stamps has proved to be successful. You can give them out quickly and easily to everybody who is working hard in your lesson. It takes a matter of seconds to stamp everybody in a small reading group. This is an additional incentive on top of verbal encouragement. Any system of reward linked to work at home is likely to lead to more reading practice taking place.

Linking praise to a specific achievement is especially effective in encouraging reluctant readers. It is important to let the pupils know what targets they are aiming for in improving their reading and to praise them when they achieve them.

Be sure to praise both successful and unsuccessful attempts. The pupils need to know that they are using the right strategy even when they get it wrong. Practising a strategy can be more important than getting the right answer.

Suggested reading improvement targets:
- thinking about what they are reading;
- noticing letter sounds;
- stopping if they make a mistake, rather than ploughing on;
- trying to work words out without asking you every time they are stuck;
- rereading a phrase to try and get it right;
- looking for a pattern they know in an unfamiliar word;
- using the pictures to help them;
- for pupils with a low concentration span, staying on task for a specific amount of time.

Some light touch phonics work

Pupils in need of a text as simple as those in *The Matt Merton Mysteries* will benefit from some light touch phonics work. They will still have poor sound to letter mapping skills (referred to as phoneme–grapheme correspondence) and the interventions you plan with them must be linked closely to the reading of *The Matt Merton Mysteries*.

Guidelines
- Keep interventions short (two to five minutes of reading group time).
- Target them at a particular problem that arises while reading a real text.
- Avoid turning a particular problem into a fully fledged phonics lesson.

Rapid segmenting and blending on a familiar text

First a reminder of what these key terms mean:
Segmenting – splitting a word into its sounds for spelling
Blending – putting a word together by moulding its sounds for reading

With familiar words
Why not take a word the pupil has read fluently from a *Matt Merton Mysteries* text and get them to segment and blend it? The pupil is already confident they can say the word, so it's a good way of practising how sounds relate to letters.

With unfamiliar words
On some occasions, the same exercises can be done with a word the pupil is finding difficult to read. Although this will cause more anxiety, it's still important to do it. Sounding out the individual phonemes in a word and blending them for reading is a vital skill. An example from *The Matt Merton Mysteries* might be: 'He could remember everything.' Sound out each letter of 'remember'. Then go on to talk about chunking or syllabification with the word 'everything' – every - thing. This is blending. 'Could' is an irregular word that needs to be learned by sight.

A segmenting exercise
The teacher says a word and the pupils try to write it by 'hearing' the individual sounds in it – they are separating the syllables or chunking.

A blending exercise
If a word cannot be read but is phonically regular, encourage blending right through the word from start to finish pronouncing each sound, as in the word 'contact' – c-o-n-t-a-c-t.

Alternatively encourage pupils to chunk words, such as 'particular' – par - ti - cu - lar – or 'everywhere' – every - where.

Introducing *The Matt Merton Mysteries* series

You will see that the first four pages of each story are the same. These introduce the place and time in which all eight books are set. It is important that you introduce these pages to the class as a whole: read them through, or ask pupils to take turns to read. Ask questions about the text and pictures to establish their comprehension of events and the place and time. For example:

Pages 4–5
- Does this look like a city today? If not, why not?
- What can you see that could be in a city today?
- What does the text tell you happened after alien spaceships crash-landed on Earth? Are the people happy? Why not?
- What does The Firm do?

Pages 6–7
- Is Matt Merton an alien? How do you know?
- What is his job?
- Is Matt happy? If not, why not?
- What do you think 'The Firm' is?

The importance of good questioning in guided reading (Based on Bloom's Taxonomy)

Teachers tend to ask questions in the 'knowledge' category most of the time, but it is important to vary questions. Here are four useful tips.

- Ask challenging questions. Avoid phrasing questions that are closed.
- Ask open-ended questions that encourage the exploration of possibilities and widen discussion.
- Ask uncluttered questions – ones that don't involve many sub-questions.
- Don't answer a question yourself after asking. Learn to wait a few moments.

KNOWLEDGE	COMPREHENSION
• remembering • memorising • recognising • recalling identification • recalling information • describing – who, what, when, where, how?	• interpreting • translating from one medium to another • describing in one's own words • organisation and selection of facts and ideas • retell …
APPLICATION	**ANALYSIS**
• problem solving • applying information to produce some result • use of facts, rules and principles • how is … an example of …? • how is … related to …? • why is … important?	• subdividing something to show how it is put together • identifying motives • separation of a whole into component parts • what are the features of …? • outline, draw a diagram … • how does … compare/contrast with …? • what evidence can you find for …?
SYNTHESIS	**EVALUATION**
• creating something new that may be in verbal form or may be a physical object • combination of ideas to form something new • what would you predict/infer from …? • what ideas can you add to …? • how would you create/design a new …? • what might happen if you …? • what solutions would you suggest for …?	• making value decisions about issues • resolving controversies or differences of opinion • development of opinions, judgements or decisions • do you agree that …? • what do you think about …? • what is the most important …? • place the following in order of importance … • how would you decide about …?

The Matt Merton Mysteries eBooks

Using electronic versions of books, eBooks, on handheld devices is a proven way of motivating and supporting less able and reluctant readers. Pupils, especially boys, love accessing books through the exciting technology that they use in other parts of their lives, making reading comparable with activities such as gaming and surfing the net.

A big advantage of using eBooks on handheld devices is the degree of privacy offered to the reader – peers cannot see which level of book pupils are reading, so there is no embarrassment about being on a book scheme aimed at younger or less able readers. This removes a major barrier to reading success. Pupils like using eBooks on handheld devices as people around them won't know if they are reading or playing an electronic game. And if a reader wants to keep rereading one title until they are comfortable to move on to another, no one need know they are still on the same book. Any potential stigma is avoided.

eBooks enable readers to choose the text size and typeface that suits them and to easily navigate books by jumping to the right chapter or page and using electronic bookmarks. Other simple-to-use tools include being able to add comments and questions to pages so that pupils can flag parts they didn't understand or particularly enjoyed. All this aids active reading and comprehension, as well as making reading enjoyable.

All eight books in *The Matt Merton Mysteries* series can be accessed as eBooks (as well as the eight *Shadows* books). Not only can they be used on PDAs, but teachers can also display them for the whole class or a guided reading group on an interactive whiteboard, PC/Mac or laptop. You can explore books together, listen to automated audio, highlight sections, add comments and more. For more details and to download your free book, go to i-Stars.co.uk.

DEADLY NIGHT

Story summary
It's late at night, but Matt can't sleep. He goes to Sam's cafe and then for a walk. He sees a light on in a school and decides to investigate. Inside he finds a boy at a computer, looking at images of Matt, Dexter and Jane. Matt interrogates the boy but gets no response. He doesn't want to use the Truth Stick on such a young boy, so instead he locks him in the classroom and calls Dexter. Dexter says he will be right over and Matt decides to wait outside on the street. Shortly afterwards a helicopter flies over the school and drops a bomb on it. Dexter calls Matt and admits to having the boy killed. The story ends with Matt feeling extremely angry at the lost opportunity to find out what the boy was doing.

Difficult words and spelling
- customer, already, routine, destroyed, disappeared, people, survive, building, following, dangerous, furniture, remember, silent, question, believe, computer, photograph, scan, hacker, middle, hacking, noise, calm, regret, helicopter, thought, suddenly, business, replied, guess, concern, knew, wouldn't
- 'ly' endings: deadly, quickly, suddenly
- Compound words: in+side, any+body, no+thing, any+way, to+night

Other language work
- Irregular past tense verbs: went, drank, tried, broke, thought, found, flew
- Apostrophes for contraction: can't, won't, didn't, don't, that's, what's
- Apostrophes for possession: mother's name
- Use of single speech marks to draw attention to a phrase – 'the look'

Questions to interrogate the text
Chapter 1
- Why do you think Matt is having trouble sleeping?
- Why is it snowing? Why are the streets empty?
- Do you think the author is building up a tense atmosphere? How is he doing this?
- What does the title of the story imply? Will something good or bad happen?
- Why does Matt break into the school?

Chapter 2
- What does Matt find in the school?
- What is strange about what is on the boy's computer?
- Why can't Matt bring himself to use the Truth Stick?

Chapter 3
- Who does Matt call for help?
- Why does Dexter address Matt by his surname, Merton?
- What does Matt tell Dexter the boy is doing? What is 'hacking'? What is he hacking into?
- Why does Matt think the boy is an Enemy?
- What does Dexter tell Matt to do?
- What happens next?

Chapter 4
- Why did Dexter have the boy killed?
- What did Matt want to do with the boy?
- Do you think Dexter expected Matt to survive the bombing? How can you tell?
- At the end of the story, why is Matt so angry?

Role-play/drama suggestions
Freeze-frame Matt and the boy in the school. What is each character thinking and feeling? What is their body language like?

Conscience alley: one pupil plays Matt; the others form two lines to make an alley. Matt is faced with the dilemma of whether or not to kill the boy with his Truth Stick. As he walks through the alley the pupils advise him what to do, giving reasons. You could ask pupils on one side to urge the Truth Stick option, and the other side to promote alternatives. At the end, Matt has to give his decision and support it with reasons.

The copymaster sheets
PCM 1 deals with skills of inference and critical thinking.
It encourages pupils to read and think critically, rather than taking all the information given by characters at face value. This task could be extended into a longer piece of writing about Matt and The Firm, written from Dexter's point of view. The writing could be specifically about what happened at the school, and why. Talk about whether Dexter expected Matt to survive the bomb blast. What clues are there in the text that he may have wanted to kill Matt?

PCM 2 focuses on creative writing skills.
It requires pupils to imagine a conversation between Matt and the boy. Pupils are asked to reread pages 18–25 and to look at the pictures for visual clues. They are given a film script structure for writing. Extra support is given with some idea prompts at the bottom of the page. Talk about whether the pupils think Matt would use the Truth Stick on someone so young. Why/why not?

All about Dexter

Name: _____   Date: _____

- Can Dexter be trusted?
- Look at what Dexter says and does in the story. Write what you think he is really thinking.

Talk about
- Did Dexter want Matt to die in the bomb blast?

Deadly Night PCM 1

Focus: Reading comprehension
RAF3: Deduce, infer or interpret information from texts

Solving the mystery

Name: _____ Date: _____

- Read pages 18 to 25 of the story and look carefully at the pictures.
- Now imagine that the boy speaks to Matt. Write what they say to each other. Use the film script started for you.
- You could use an idea from the box.
- You will need another sheet of paper.

Matt	Look, I don't want to use this Truth Stick. Just tell me who you work for and what you are doing.
Boy	Well, I ...

Ideas

The boy is working for The Firm.

The boy is spying on Dexter, Matt and Jane.

The boy is working with Jane against The Firm.

The boy was hacking into the school computers and accidentally found secret files about The Firm.

- Would Matt use the Truth Stick on someone so young?

Deadly Night PCM 2

Focus: Reading comprehension
WAF1: Write imaginative, interesting and thoughtful texts

SET UP

Story summary
Matt is in Sam's cafe when he gets an urgent text from Dexter. He and Dexter rush off to stop a bomb attack on the clock tower. On arriving they see a woman running up the stairs of the tower. Matt calls out for her to stop but she ignores him. He gives chase and Dexter falls behind. After a tussle the woman takes out a Truth Stick and Matt recognises her as someone who has tried to kill him before. Dexter finally comes to the rescue but the woman escapes past him. Dexter is evasive when Matt asks him where he was. Back in Sam's cafe, Matt mulls over what has happened and realises that his life is increasingly in danger.

Difficult words and spelling
- depressed, world, staring, remembered, customer, were/where, would, supposed, dangerous, people, laughed, tower, through, knew, right, centre, bomb, familiar, thought, reached, pointing, lower, purpose, business
- Double consonants: coffee, better, supposed, attack, suffer, running, fell, dizzy, grabbed, dropped, carefully, happens, getting
- 'y' at end of a word as an 'ee' sound: every, city, quickly, hurry, Enemy, happy, lucky
- Split o-e phoneme: alone, drove, closer
- Split i-e phoneme: time, chime, smiled
- 'ea'/'ear' sounds: fear, learn, reached, meant
- 'ou' phoneme: outside, clouds, loud, round, shouted (compare to: you, would, through, four)

Other language work
- Speech punctuation
- Use of exclamation marks: 'Dexter, I need back-up!'
- Onomatopoeia: dong (clock chimes)
- Ellipsis: … there was fear in their eyes

Questions to interrogate the text
Chapter 1
- What does the title of the book mean? Who do you think will be set up?
- Do Matt and Sam know each other well? How can you tell?
- What do you think 'Code Red' in the text message means?
- Does Dexter like Matt? How can you tell?
- What is the Code Red about?
- How do people react to Matt and Dexter? Why?

Chapter 2
- Why does Matt have to put his hands over his ears?
- The book says Dexter could not keep up. Could there be another reason why he falls behind?
- What does Matt notice about the woman when he sees her up close?
- How does the woman get past Dexter? Do you think Dexter could do more to stop her?

Chapter 3
- Does Matt believe that Dexter couldn't manage the stairs? What does he think Dexter is up to?
- How do the events in the clock tower relate to the title of the book?
- What just happened to Matt isn't uncommon. How do we know this from Matt's conversation with Sam?
- How do you think Matt now feels about Dexter and The Firm?
- Is the ending a good one? Talk about ending on a cliffhanger and how the author has built up suspense about what will happen next to Matt.

Role-play/drama suggestions
Hotseat the teacher in role as Dexter. Can the pupils get to the bottom of what Dexter was doing in the clock tower, and why? Discuss his possible body language (evasive, shrugging shoulders, not making eye contact).

Freeze-frame the woman pointing a Truth Stick at Matt, with Dexter off to one side. Tap each character and ask them what they are thinking.

The copymaster sheets
PCM 1 deals with recall and sequencing skills.
The correct order of the events is 3, 5, 2, 6, 1, 4. The pupils could cut out the events and glue them in a line on another piece of paper, so that a bar graph can be drawn beneath, plotting tension and excitement in the story. Talk about what the pupils think is the most exciting point in the story. Discuss how the tension builds to the moment when Matt recognises the woman, and then falls away as she escapes.

PCM 2 asks the pupils to use skills of inference and deduction.
Pupils look back through the book and analyse the clues that indicate Matt has been set up (by Dexter). They should write short notes explaining what each clue could mean. Page numbers could be removed from the sheet to make it more challenging. If pupils have read *Shadows: Under Fire* they will know that the woman used to work for The Firm and has tried to kill Matt before. Talk about why Dexter is trying to kill Matt, and raise the idea that The Firm might think Matt knows too much (he suspects that The Firm are bad, and possibly on the side of the aliens).

Order it

Name: _____ Date: _____

- Look at the time line for the book.
- Match the events to the time line.

Start of the book ⟶ End of the book

3					

1. The woman pushes past Dexter.

2. The clock chimes and the woman pushes Matt down the stairs.

3. Matt gets a text.

4. Matt goes back to Sam's cafe.

5. Matt chases a woman in the clock tower.

6. The woman points a Truth Stick at Matt.

Talk about
- What do you think is the most exciting point in the story? Why?
- Give each event a score out of ten to show how exciting it is. (One is not very exciting and ten is very exciting.)

Set Up PCM 1

Focus: Reading comprehension/narrative tension
RAF4: Identify and comment on structure of texts

© Rising Stars UK Ltd. 2010   You may photocopy this page

Be a detective

Name: _____ Date: _____

There are five clues in the book that show Matt was set up.

- Write in the boxes what you think each clue tells you.

Clue 1
Dexter lags behind.
(page 25)

Clue 2
The woman has a Truth Stick, not a bomb.
(page 33)

Clue 3
The woman has tried to kill Matt before.
(page 34)

Clue 4
The woman smiles at Dexter and escapes.
(page 37)

Clue 5
Dexter looks away.
(page 38)

Talk about
- Who set Matt up? Why?

Set Up PCM 2

Focus: Reading comprehension
RAF2: Retrieve information from texts
RAF3: Deduce, infer or interpret information from texts

© Rising Stars UK Ltd. 2010 You may photocopy this page

THE WARNING

Story summary
The story begins with Matt receiving an email from his boss, telling him and Dexter to go to a seaside town to find The Enemy. They investigate every house there, without success. Dexter thinks The Enemy must be hiding, but Matt disagrees; he thinks the people they have met are just scared of The Firm. Matt walks off. He decides to leave The Firm for good and thinks he can hack into their files to find Jane. Later that night Matt sees Dexter and The Firm on the beach killing all the men and women from the town. Then a man changes into an alien, while Dexter and the others kneel before him. Matt flees back to the city, more certain than ever that he has to stop The Firm and their alien masters.

Difficult words and spelling
- bombs, where/were, factory, destroy, often, silence, advice, thought, laughed, questions, people, tip off, script, coward, traitor, leave, expecting, spies, knew, while, skimmed, hack, restless, middle, right, raised, voice, murder, kneel, reception, alley, believe, lies, peace, world
- Irregular 'or' sound: work, worst, world
- Dropping final 'e' when adding 'ing' suffix: hiding, coming
- to/too

Other language work
- Pronouns: singular him, he; plural them, they
- Vivid verbs: scared, love, laughed, skimmed, killed, shocked
- Imperative verbs – giving commands: Grow up; Come back; Send me

Questions to interrogate the text
Chapter 1
- What job does Matt's boss give him to do?
- From their conversation, how can you tell that Matt and Dexter don't like each other?

Chapter 2
- How do Matt and Dexter check the houses?
- What is Dexter's reaction to not finding The Enemy?
- What is Matt's reaction?
- What does Dexter do when Matt leaves?
- What does Matt do next? What important decisions does he make?

Chapter 3
- What does Matt witness on the beach at night?
- How does the author show that Dexter doesn't give the people a chance to show they are innocent?
- How does the author show Matt's reaction with a description of body language?
- What is the shocking revelation that Matt sees next?
- Can you tell what the alien's relationship is to the people in The Firm?

Chapter 4
- What does Matt read in the news the next day?
- Is the news report true?
- At the end of the story, what does Matt decide he must do?

Role-play/drama suggestions
Use the 'Stop the clock' technique. Create a role-play of Dexter lining up people on the beach and Matt looking on in horror. Tell the rest of the group that at any moment, one of them can shout 'Stop!' and freeze the action. That person may then swap places with one of the role-play characters and act or speak in a way that changes the outcome of the scene. Can Matt do/say something to persuade Dexter to stop?

Role-play Matt confronting the alien leader just after he has witnessed the innocent people on the beach being killed. What might they say/do to one another?

The copymaster sheets
PCM 1 looks at character traits.
It requires pupils to select appropriate vocabulary to describe the characters of Matt and Dexter. Some of the words and phrases are quite challenging to read and understand. You can differentiate this activity by using only simple words, or by asking pupils to think of their own descriptive vocabulary. Talk about why both characters can be described as angry: Matt is angry with Dexter and The Firm for the terrible things that they do, whereas Dexter seems to be a generally angry person who takes out his anger on the people around him. Also discuss how the author shows the reader what each character is like – through actions, dialogue, pictures and descriptions.

PCM 2 invites pupils to write a newspaper report.
A template is provided with a headline, subheading and opening sentence. Pupils are prompted to cover the five Ws (what, when, who, where, why) and to include a quote. You can reinforce work on the newspaper/report genre by discussing key features such as headline, introduction, paragraphs, eyewitness quotes and so on. Talk about how Matt must have felt when he read the false newspaper report that covered up what really happened at the beach.

Matt and Dexter

Name: _____ Date: _____

- Choose words and phrases to describe Matt and Dexter. Write them under their pictures.
- Two have been done for you.
- Which word matches both characters?

> nice   nasty   kind   caring   angry   hurtful
> sympathetic   bossy   questions things   scared   worried
> follows orders without thinking

Matt	Dexter
nice	nasty

- How do the characters' actions in the story show what they are like? On the back of this sheet, write sentences using the words you have chosen.
- An example is given below.

> Dexter is a **nasty** person because when Matt talks about happy memories of the seaside, Dexter laughs at him and is mean to him.

- How does the author show what each character is like?

The Warning PCM 1

Focus: Describe and write about character traits
RAF3: Deduce, infer or interpret information or ideas from texts
WAF7: Select appropriate and effective vocabulary

© Rising Stars UK Ltd. 2010   You may photocopy this page

Front page news

Name: _____ Date: _____

In Chapter 4 Matt reads a newspaper report of what happened at the beach. He knows that the story is false.

- Write a newspaper report of what really happened at the beach. It has been started for you.
- Try to cover the five Ws: <u>W</u>hat happened? <u>W</u>hen? <u>W</u>ho? <u>W</u>here? <u>W</u>hy?
- Include a quote from Matt.

TOWN WIPED OUT BY THE FIRM

Can The Firm be trusted?

Last night a whole town of people was killed by The Firm. Matt Merton, who works for The Firm, saw what happened.

Talk about
- How does Matt feel when he reads the false newspaper report that covers up what really happened?

The Warning PCM 2

Focus: Write a newspaper report
WAF2: Produce texts appropriate to task, reader and purpose
WAF3: Organise and present whole texts effectively

THE NIGHTMARE

Story summary
The story begins with Matt waking up from a terrible nightmare about the night of The Crash. He makes an effort to recall the dream and types it up on his computer. The events of the night of The Crash are revealed: Matt was taken by aliens to their spaceship, along with other strong healthy people. They became the organisation known as The Firm. Before their eyes, the aliens took on human form and gave out Truth Sticks, ordering The Firm to kill the young and the old, and anyone else who got in their way. Matt realises with horror that ever since that night he has been killing innocent people on the aliens' orders. The next morning, Matt goes to Sam's cafe and decides that he has to stay in The Firm so that he can find Jane as soon as possible.

Difficult words and spelling
- middle, sweat, people, knew, thought, world, believed, fuel, supply, would, memory, remember, hours, buildings, noise, confusion, computer, type, laser, explosion, photographs, vitamin, exact, impossible, resists, realised, questions, control, dreadful, freedom, right, usual
- 'or' and 'er' endings: mirror, traitor, customer
- Compound words: night+mare, girl+friend, key+board, any+one, every+thing, to+day

Other language work
- Irregular past tense verbs: woke, got, went, found, gave, took, made, told, grew (compare to regular 'ed' endings: looked, called)
- Apostrophes for missing letters: you're/you are; couldn't/could not

Questions to interrogate the text
Chapter 1
- Why is it always snowing?
- What was Matt's dream about? What has he forgotten?
- How does Matt make sure he will remember his dream?

Chapter 2
- Where did the aliens take Matt?
- What sort of people did the aliens take? Why?
- What is The Firm?
- What did the aliens give Matt and the others?
- What did the aliens command Matt and the others to do? Why?
- What strange thing did the aliens do to themselves? Why?
- What terrible thing has Matt been doing since he joined The Firm? Why?
- Is Matt completely sure about what happened on the night of The Crash? How can you tell?

Chapter 3
- Why does hardly anybody go into Sam's cafe anymore?
- Why does Matt decide to stay with The Firm?

Role-play/drama suggestions
Role-play Matt being taken by the aliens and being made to join The Firm. Consider the emotions he would be going through.

Imagine you are filming the book for a TV programme. How would you direct Matt having his nightmare? Think about actions such as tossing and turning; a perspiring forehead/body; props such as crumpled sheets; dramatic lighting and music. Can you recreate the scene effectively?

The copymaster sheets
PCM 1 assesses comprehension, asking pupils to pick out facts which reveal the truth about The Firm.
Statements b, c, d, f and g are true. This is quite a tricky exercise and the statements need to be read carefully. To help pupils, clarify the cover story put out by The Firm (that they are fighting the aliens) and the truth (they are working for the aliens). Encourage pupils to use the visual clues on the sheet and in the book. Talk about the untrue statements and find evidence in the book that disproves them.

PCM 2 deals with recall and issues of empathy with the character of Matt.
Pupils are asked to compose an email from Matt to Jane, explaining what happened on the night of The Crash and how he feels about it. Support is given with a vocabulary box; you could cover this up to make the activity more challenging. Check understanding of the trickier words like 'guilty' with the group. This task is ideal for an extended piece of descriptive/recount writing and the email format may help to encourage reluctant writers. Talk about how Matt feels about his work for The Firm, and how difficult it will be for him to continue in his job, now that he knows the truth. Consider his motivation to stay in The Firm (to find Jane).

The truth about The Firm

Name: _____ Date: _____

- This is what Matt is told, but he's not sure if it's true.

> The Firm keeps people safe.

> The Firm fights the aliens.

- Draw lines to <u>five</u> boxes that are true. One has been done for you.

a. Matt helped people escape on the night of The Crash.

b. The aliens took strong humans and called them The Firm.

c. The aliens gave The Firm Truth Sticks.

d. The aliens trained The Firm to kill people.

e. The Firm only kills people on the side of the aliens.

f. Matt has been helping the aliens by killing people.

g. The aliens gave The Firm drugs to control them.

Talk about
- Which sentences are not true? Find evidence from the book.

The Nightmare PCM 1

Focus: Reading comprehension
RAF2: Retrieve information from texts
RAF3: Deduce, infer or interpret information from texts

© Rising Stars UK Ltd. 2010   You may photocopy this page

Matt remembers

Name: _____ Date: _____

- Imagine you are Matt. Write an email to Jane, telling her that you remember what happened on the night of The Crash.
- Write about your feelings in the email. You could use words from the box.
- The email has been started for you.

| upset angry scared guilty sad ashamed uncertain worried |

From: Matt
To: Jane
Subject: Night of The Crash

Sent: 06/11/2021 02.15am

Dear Jane
I can remember what happened to me on the night of The Crash. It all came back to me in a terrible nightmare.

Talk about
- Now that Matt knows the truth about his job, can he keep working for The Firm?

The Nightmare PCM 2

Focus: Writing a recount/explanation/letter
WAF1: Write imaginative, interesting and thoughtful texts
WAF7: Select appropriate and effective vocabulary

THE TRAP

Story summary
Matt wants to leave The Firm but he has to stay so that he can find his girlfriend, Jane, before The Firm does. Meanwhile, Dexter's boss is angry that Dexter has let his personal feelings get in the way of doing his job. The alien leader has Dexter taken away and killed, then vows to kill Matt and Jane itself. Matt gets a text from Jane and goes to meet her. She seems taller than before and her eyes and hands seem different too. It turns out to be a trap – the alien leader has disguised itself as Jane. The alien reverts to its true form and snaps Matt's Truth Stick, which emits a shrill noise causing the alien to shake. Matt escapes and heads for the relative safety of Sam's cafe. The two men are worried about what the future holds but take comfort in their friendship.

Difficult words and spelling
- danger, believed, protecting, world, knew, leave, would, survive, questions, target, voice, enough, excuses, contact, defeat, perfume, remembered, squeezed, memory, recently, confused, creatures, slaves, against, shrill, noise, gained, strength, followed, company
- Homophones: their/there
- Compound words: girl+friend, no+thing, my+self, over+joyed, in+to, can+not, some+body

Other language work
- Comparatives: taller, stronger, bigger
- Vivid verbs: killed, squeezed, snapped, shake, trapped, scared

Questions to interrogate the text
Chapter 1
- Thinking about the title, can you predict what might happen in this story?
- Why does Matt have to stay in The Firm?
- What did Dexter's boss want him to do?
- How many times has Dexter tried to kill Matt?
- What happens to Dexter? How can you tell?

Chapter 2
- When and where does Matt meet Jane?
- What signs are there that it is always winter?
- What clues suggest that Matt should be wary of Jane?
- Explain why Jane tells Matt: 'You have seen their leader.'
- Can you explain the book's title now?

Chapter 3
- How do you think Matt feels, seeing Jane turn into the alien leader?
- What does the alien leader do to Matt's Truth Stick?
- How does the broken Truth Stick help Matt escape?

Chapter 4
- Where does Matt go to feel safe? Why?

Role-play/drama suggestions
Role-play Matt meeting the disguised alien leader: Jane acting strangely, Matt trying to work out what is wrong, and then the moment of revelation. You could try a silent tableau to allow pupils to focus on body language, facial expression and movement. Pupils could be asked to find a suitable piece of dramatic music to accompany the tableau, or to create their own soundtrack using instruments. The moment when the Truth Stick snaps is perfect for combining movement and sound effects.

Imagine that Dexter has been imprisoned by the aliens and is awaiting punishment. Either hotseat Dexter to explore how he feels, or role-play Matt finding Dexter and confronting him. Would Matt help Dexter escape? Would Dexter accept Matt's help? Explore themes of regret and forgiveness.

The copymaster sheets
PCM 1 considers basic story structure.
Pupils are asked to separate the story into four parts, writing notes about each and adding page references. You could use this sheet as a discussion activity and complete the story mountain together. Talk about how the story is only partly resolved. Matt manages to escape from the alien leader this time – but the story ends with tension, as Matt and Sam wait for more terrible events to unfold.

PCM 2 is a true or false activity involving reading comprehension.
Answers: 1 – false (p8); 2 – false (p12); 3 – true (p21); 4 – true (p29); 5 – false (p34); 6 – true (p40). Statement 5 is tricky and could be a starting point for further discussion: although the alien leader says the Truth Stick is 'useless' and snaps it, the shrill noise it makes prevents the alien from moving. Talk about what the pupils think the real Jane is up to and how she would feel about being used as 'bait' to trap Matt.

Story mountain

Name: _____ Date: _____

- Stories usually have four parts.
- Look carefully at *The Trap*. Can you find these four parts in the story?
- On each part of the mountain write a few words about the story. Give the page numbers.

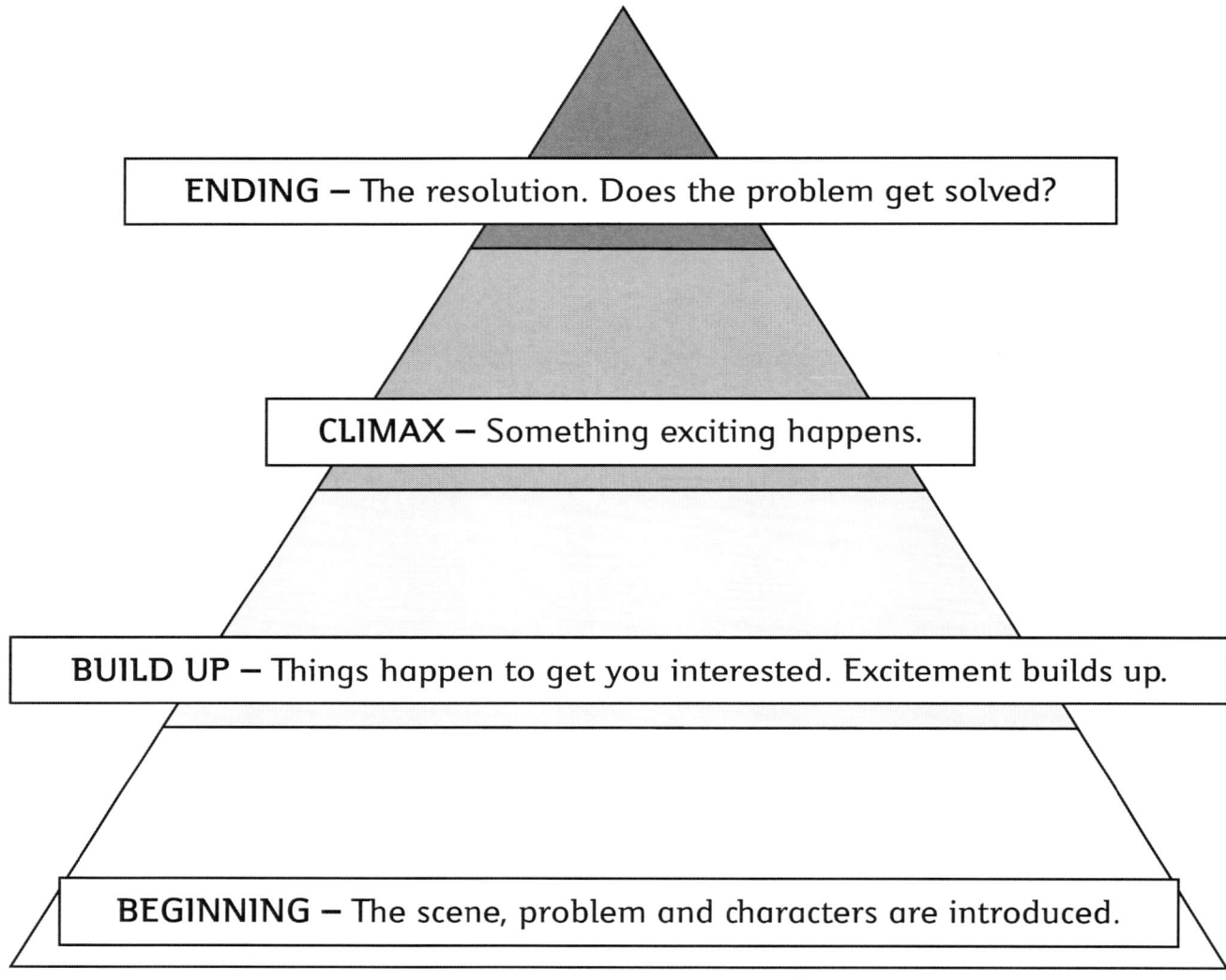

ENDING – The resolution. Does the problem get solved?

CLIMAX – Something exciting happens.

BUILD UP – Things happen to get you interested. Excitement builds up.

BEGINNING – The scene, problem and characters are introduced.

Talk about
- At the end of this book, is Matt's story over? What questions have not been answered?

The Trap PCM 1

Focus: Story structure
RAF4: Identify and comment on the structure of texts

© Rising Stars UK Ltd. 2010

You may photocopy this page

True or false?

Name: _____ Date: _____

- Say whether these statements are true (✓) or false (✗).
- In the spaces, write words from the book that prove this.

	True or false?
1. Matt decides he must leave The Firm.	
2. Dexter's boss is pleased with him.	
3. It is very cold.	
4. The alien leader sets a trap for Matt.	
5. The Truth Stick cannot harm the alien leader.	
6. Sam is worried about Matt.	

- How do you think Jane would feel about the alien leader pretending to be her?

The Trap PCM 2

Focus: Reading comprehension
RAF2: Retrieve information from texts
RAF3: Deduce, infer or interpret information from texts

The Matt Merton Mysteries Teacher's Book

CHANGING SIDES

Story summary
The story begins with two men from The Firm walking into Sam's cafe, looking for Matt. They question Sam and threaten him with a Truth Stick. When Matt comes in later, Sam urges him to leave through the back door. Matt gets on the sky tram and realises two men are following him. Then he gets a text from Jane, asking him to meet her. Matt jumps into a car and manages to lose the men. He is reunited with Jane, who explains that she has been watching him, and that it wasn't safe for them to meet up until Matt realised that The Firm was evil. Jane says they must work together to stop aliens taking over the world. Just then the two men reappear and Matt and Jane hide. They agree to meet up later to carry out Jane's plan.

Difficult words and spelling
- agents, customers, protect, disappeared, lie, knew, reached, glared, understand, against, reflection, following, trouble, lose, forced, thought, suddenly, believe, survival, flagged, would, squeezed, because, remember, drugged, slave, world
- Homophones: two/too
- Irregular sound for 'a': walked, watched (compare to: man, cafe, ran)
- Compare 'ea'/'ear' sounds: deadly, hear, early, reached, breath, fear, ready, leave, mean, read

Other language work
- Question marks: Has Matt Merton been in here today?
- Vivid verbs: grabbed, glared, forced, jumped, missed, squeezed, killed

Questions to interrogate the text
Chapter 1
- Think about the title, *Changing Sides*. Can you predict what this story might be about?
- How does Sam feel about the two men who come into his cafe and ask questions about Matt?

Chapter 2
- What does Sam do when Matt comes into the cafe?
- What transport does Matt use first?
- How does the author make you feel when Matt is being followed?
- What does Jane say in her text message?
- How does Matt get away from the two men?
- Why does Matt tell the driver not to look at his face?

Chapter 3
- What is Matt's initial reaction to Jane? Why is he uncertain?
- Why has Jane waited until now to meet up with Matt?
- What does Jane want Matt to help her with?
- What plans do they make when they reach Sam's cafe?
- How do you think Matt feels when he and Jane say goodbye?
- How effective is the last sentence: 'And they each ran into the shadows of the dark city, alone.'

Role-play/drama suggestions
Use the flashback technique: focus on Jane and ask pupils to imagine what has been happening in her life prior to the meeting with Matt. You could pinpoint three different times: before The Crash, a few days after The Crash, and a few hours before the meeting. If pupils have read *The Trap*, you could focus on Matt and his concerns that Jane may not be who she says she is.

Role-play the scene where Sam is threatened by the two men from The Firm. Think about body language – intimidating/frightened. Can Sam convince the men that he doesn't know about Matt's work?

The copymaster sheets
PCM 1 considers the characters of Matt and Jane.
It requires pupils to decide which thought/feeling statements match either Matt or Jane, and to find the two statements that apply to both. (Answers: Matt – b, e, g; Jane – c, d, h; both – a, f.) Pupils may have slightly different answers and this is fine as long as they can justify them. Talk about the reasons why Jane has kept away from Matt until now. Discuss why it wasn't safe to approach Matt while he worked for and believed in The Firm. What is different now? Draw out that Jane has known the truth for a lot longer than Matt, and that she has been spying on him, in the hope that he would discover the truth for himself. Examine the risks that both characters are taking by meeting up, and by deciding to fight against The Firm.

PCM 2 considers Sam's dilemma.
Pupils are asked to write a letter from Sam to Matt, explaining why he can no longer help him. Encourage them to link up the points in their letter using simple connectives, e.g. Sam cannot help Matt **because** he is too scared, **but** he is very sorry about this. Talk about what the pupils would do if they were Sam. If they have read *Shadows: Night of the Crash* they can draw on their knowledge that Sam lost his own family that night but bravely saved many others.

The meeting

Name: _____ Date: _____

- Matt and Jane finally meet in *Changing Sides*. How do they feel?
- Below are some of their thoughts. Draw lines to match the thoughts to the correct character.
- Tip: two of the statements match <u>both</u> Matt and Jane.

a. I have really missed you.

b. Can it really be you?

c. I have been watching you.

d. It hasn't been safe until now.

e. I didn't know where you were.

f. I want to stop The Firm.

g. Why haven't you been in touch?

h. I wish you didn't work for The Firm.

- Write one more thought or feeling for each character.

Matt: _____

Jane: _____

- Was Jane right to keep away from Matt until now?

Changing Sides PCM 1

Focus: Empathise with a character
RAF3: Deduce, infer or interpret information or ideas from texts

Sam's story

Name: _____ Date: _____

- Sam is worried. He wants to help Matt, but he is scared of The Firm.
- Imagine you are Sam and write a letter to Matt.
- Include these points in your letter:

| Sam is sorry. | He cannot help Matt or be friends with him anymore. | He is too scared. |

Sam's cafe
11/12/2021

Dear Matt,

Talk about

- If you were Sam, would you decide to help Matt? Why/why not?

Changing Sides PCM 2

Focus: Examine a dilemma/Write a letter
RAF3: Deduce, infer or interpret information or ideas from texts
WAF2: Produce texts appropriate to task and purpose

© Rising Stars UK Ltd. 2010

You may photocopy this page

THE END: PART ONE

Story summary
The Firm has burnt down Sam's cafe, but Jane saved Matt and Sam from the fire. They have fled to another cafe where two men from The Firm come in looking for Matt. Jane drives Matt and Sam to some woods and explains that it is always cold because the aliens have built a shield that blocks the Sun's rays. As the Earth becomes colder and darker, humans will die out and the aliens will thrive. Jane then talks about Route 6 – a place where drugged prisoners work at computers to keep the shield in place. Her plan is to kill the alien leader and destroy the main computer, bringing down the shield so that all the aliens are destroyed by the Sun's light and heat. The prisoners have stopped taking their drugs and are ready to help. Matt is relieved that he can put his experience working for The Firm to good use in fighting the aliens.

Difficult words and spelling
- remembered, would, memory, thought, safety, through, fought, knew, world, photo, calm, nervous, shivered, pointed, reason, during, building, shield, Earth, control, confusion, survivors, route, people, against, prisoners, drugged, computer, destroy, dangerous, laughed, squeezed, freedom
- Capital letters for important nouns: the Earth, Route 6, The Firm, and people's names

Other language work
- Question marks: Are we safe? What can you see?
- Plural pronouns: She pulled them to safety; They drove through the night.

Questions to interrogate the text
Chapter 1
- Why aren't Matt, Jane and Sam in Sam's cafe?
- What has Matt learnt about The Firm?
- Why do Jane, Matt and Sam leave the cafe in a hurry?

Chapter 2
- Where does Jane drive Matt and Sam?
- What is strange about the sky?
- Why has it been so cold since The Crash?
- Why do the aliens want it to be cold and dark?

Chapter 3
- What place does Jane tell them about?
- What do the aliens use Route 6 for? What do the prisoners do there?
- What plan does Jane have for destroying the aliens?
- What does Jane think will help them succeed?

Role-play/drama suggestions
Role-play the prisoners in Route 6 talking to each other. How do they feel? How did they get there? What is it like to sit at a computer all day and all night? Have they made any plans to escape, or do they feel hopeless? Think about how they would move and act – huddled together, shivering from the cold, nervous and jumpy, etc.

Freeze-frame the moment when Jane tells Matt and Sam about the alien shield and its effects. Jane could be pointing at the sky while Matt and Sam look up. Think about facial expressions that show how the characters are feeling. Tap each character on the shoulder and ask them what they are thinking and feeling.

The copymaster sheets
PCM 1 deals with 'reading' visual clues and skills of recall.
It requires pupils to look at a series of images from the book, including flashbacks to earlier stories, and to pick out the dangers faced by Matt, Jane and Sam as they fight The Firm. As this worksheet is open-ended and uses visual clues, it should be very accessible to learners. However, recall and text comprehension skills are also needed to fully understand the images. Talk about what Matt, Jane and Sam are risking to fight The Firm: their safety, the safety of people close to them, Matt's job, Sam's livelihood and, ultimately, their lives.

PCM 2 tackles persuasive writing.
The pupils are asked to write a note from Jane to the prisoners in Route 6, persuading them to risk their lives to help her bring down the shield and defeat the aliens. The boxed words and phrases could be covered up to make the activity more challenging. This writing task is suitable for any ability level as the blank space lets pupils write as much as they feel they can. To support less able pupils, you could discuss ideas before they start writing. Share the pupils' work: which notes are particularly persuasive and why? Talk about whether the pupils would help Jane if they were prisoners in Route 6.

Danger! Danger!

Name: _____ Date: _____

- Look at the pictures below from the story.
- Pick out the details that show the dangers that Matt, Sam and Jane face. Write these around the pictures.
- One has been done for you.

| Matt is always on the run. | | They are looking for him so they can kill him. |

| He has to hide from The Firm. | | |

- How much are Matt, Jane and Sam risking to fight The Firm?
- Would you fight The Firm if you were them? Why/Why not?

The End: Part 1 PCM 1

Focus: Reading comprehension
RAF2: Understand and describe information or events from texts
WAF7: Select appropriate and effective vocabulary

© Rising Stars UK Ltd. 2010   You may photocopy this page

Do the right thing

Name: _____ Date: _____

- Imagine you are Jane. You need to persuade the prisoners in Route 6 to help you fight the aliens.
- Write a secret note to the prisoners. Tell them your plan and give reasons why they should help you.
- You could use words and phrases from the box.

> please   we must
> if we don't defeat the aliens then ...
> save the world   brave
> cannot stand by and do nothing
> work together   the right thing to do

TOP SECRET!   Please read, then pass on

Talk about
- Would you help Jane if you were a prisoner in Route 6? Why/why not?

The End: Part 1 PCM 2

Focus: Persuasive writing
WAF1: Write imaginative, interesting and thoughtful texts
WAF7: Select appropriate and effective vocabulary

The Matt Merton Mysteries Teacher's Book

THE END: PART TWO

Story summary
Matt, Jane and Sam sneak into Route 6, ready to put their plan into action and defeat the aliens. The prisoners are sitting at computers in silence. When an alien spots the intruders Matt snaps his Truth Stick so that its shrill noise immobilises the aliens. The prisoners respond by attacking the aliens. Meanwhile, Matt, Jane and Sam go to the main computer room to confront the alien leader. It grabs Jane and Sam but Matt smashes the computer, disabling the shield. The alien leader starts to burn in the sunlight. Soon it is destroyed, along with all the other aliens. The world is safe. We next see the characters four months later. Matt and Jane are celebrating their engagement at Sam's new cafe. It is spring and the world is warm and sunny once more.

Difficult words and spelling
- dawn, route, shivered, hours, prisoners, people, squeezed, knew, guard, world, frightened, computer, shield, would, forbidden, gleaming, shrill, noise, panicked, high-pitched, silent, state, fought, freedom, glowed, followed, obey, replied, reached, twitch, destroy, brighter, lighter, melting, sagged, creatures, believe, effort, skiing, celebration, diamond, blossom
- Compound words: sun+glasses, every+one, up+stairs, sun+shine, every+where

Other language work
- Irregular past tense verbs: went, drove, were, hid, took, sat, came, stood, ran, fought (compare to regular 'ed' endings: jumped, attacked)
- Vivid verbs: roared, grabbed, panicked, shake, attacked, glowed, sagged
- Onomatopoeia: shiver, snap, slam, smash, twitch

Questions to interrogate the text
Chapter 1
- Why are Matt, Jane and Sam going to Route 6?
- How do they get into Route 6?
- Why are the trucks full of people?
- Why do you think Sam says, 'This is mad'?

Chapter 2
- 'There was no sound inside Route 6.' What effect does this description have?
- What are the computers for?
- What does Matt do to harm the aliens?
- What other effect does breaking the Truth Stick have?

Chapter 3
- Where do Matt, Jane and Sam go next? Why?
- How does Matt defeat the alien leader?
- What effect does sunlight have on the aliens?
- Would you describe Matt as a hero? What about Sam and Jane?

Chapter 4
- How much time has passed since the aliens were defeated?
- Where are Matt, Jane and Sam?
- What is the weather like? Why is this significant?
- Did you notice what Jane asked to drink in the cafe? Why is this humorous?
- What do you think of the ending?

Role-play/drama suggestions
Role-play Matt, Jane and Sam confronting the alien leader in the main computer room. Create tension using sound effects or dramatic pieces of music, choreographing each character's movement in time with the music.

Hot-seat a prisoner freed by Matt, Jane and Sam. Did they immediately get up and fight, or did they hesitate? What did it feel like to fight back? Did any of their friends get hurt or killed? What would they say to Matt, Jane and Sam if they saw them again?

The copymaster sheets
PCM 1 looks at ways of setting the scene.
Pupils revisit Chapters 1 and 4 to find words that describe the setting. They are then asked to write about how each setting makes them feel and how it fits with the story. You might want to do the second part after group discussion. Talk about how the sunshine and blossom reflect the happy ending, compared with the cold, dark beginning highlighting the unhappiness and hopelessness of the prisoners. Draw out that authors (and film/television directors) often use contrasts like this for effect.

PCM 2 involves writing a newspaper report.
To extend this task you could ask pupils to use their completed planning template to write up a neat version, using ICT skills if possible, to look like a real newspaper report. As an alternative, pupils could retell the story as a comic book sequence, using simple sentences and adding dialogue in speech bubbles. Talk about the kinds of stories that typically appear on the front pages of newspapers (disasters, crime, celebrity news, etc) and discuss why newspapers choose exciting/attention-grabbing stories – to hook readers and make them want to buy the newspaper. What kind of story is their report? (An amazing tale of heroism.) Do they think newspapers carry more 'bad news' than 'good news'?

Setting the scene

Name: _____ Date: _____

- Look back at Chapter 1 and find words that tell you about the setting and weather. Write them in the chart.
- Then do the same for Chapter 4.
- Complete the rest of the chart.

Chapter 1: setting words	Chapter 4: setting words
How the setting makes me feel:	How the setting makes me feel:
Why the setting suits this part of the story:	Why the setting suits this part of the story:

Talk about
- Do you think this is a good ending to the story? Why/Why not?

The End: Part 2 PCM 1

Focus: Reading comprehension – settings
RAF2: Understand, describe, select or retrieve information from texts
RAF3: Deduce, infer or interpret information from texts

© Rising Stars UK Ltd. 2010 You may photocopy this page

Read all about it!

Name: _____ Date: _____

- Write a news report of how the aliens were defeated at Route 6.
- Include the facts and make it exciting for your readers.

Headline: (Short, grabs attention and tells readers what the news story is about)

Opening sentence: (An introduction to the news story)

What happened? Where and when? Who was involved?

Why did it happen?

Closing sentence: (Sums up the news story and answers any more questions that the reader might have)

- What kinds of stories do newspapers have on their front covers? Why?

The End: Part 2 PCM 2

Focus: Write a newspaper report
WAF2: Produce texts appropriate to task, reader and purpose
WAF3: Organise and present whole texts effectively

© Rising Stars UK Ltd. 2010

You may photocopy this page